All About Animals

What's a MAMMAL?

Anna Kaspar

PowerKiDS
press™

New York

Published in 2012 by The Rosen Publishing Group, Inc.
29 East 21st Street, New York, NY 10010

First Edition

Editor: Amelie von Zumbusch
Book Design: Ashley Drago

Photo Credits: Cover, pp. 4, 11, 12, 15, 20 Shutterstock.com; p. 7 © www.iStockphoto.com/ Dirk Freder; p. 8 © www.iStockphoto.com/Derek Dammann; pp. 16–17 David B. Fleetham/Getty Images; p. 19 © www.iStockphoto.com/Hagit Berkovich; p. 23 © www.iStockphoto.com/John Pitcher; p. 24 (bamboo) Brand X Pictures/Thinkstock.

Library of Congress Cataloging-in-Publication Data

Kaspar, Anna.
  What's a mammal? / by Anna Kaspar. — 1st ed.
      p. cm. — (All about animals)
  Includes index.
  ISBN 978-1-4488-6137-8 (library binding) — ISBN 978-1-4488-6232-0 (pbk.) — ISBN 978-1-4488-6233-7 (6-pack)
  1. Mammals—Juvenile literature. I. Title.
  QL706.2.K37 2012
  599—dc23
                                        2011017107

Manufactured in the United States of America

CPSIA Compliance Information: Batch #WW12PK: For Further Information contact Rosen Publishing, New York, New York at 1-800-237-9932

Contents

You are a mammal! Cats, dogs, cows, and bears are mammals, too.

Mammals are a kind of animal. Cheetahs are the fastest mammals.

Every mammal has at least a little hair. **Orangutans** have lots of hair!

All baby mammals drink their mothers' milk. Milk helps them grow up strong.

Mother **platypuses** lay eggs. Most mammals give birth to their babies, though.

Some mammals live in groups. A group of lions is called a pride.

Blue whales are the biggest mammals. In fact, they are the biggest animals ever!

Mammals can be found in many places. Fennec foxes live in the Sahara.

Some mammals eat plants.
Pandas eat **bamboo**.

Other mammals eat animals. **Walruses** eat mostly clams.

WORDS TO KNOW

bamboo   orangutan   platypus   walrus

INDEX

WEB SITES

Due to the changing nature of Internet links, PowerKids Press has developed an online list of Web sites related to the subject of this book. This site is updated regularly. Please use this link to access the list:
www.powerkidslinks.com/aaa/mammal/